Bridge Pamphlet
No. 10

The Rainbow Faults

Kate Wakeling grew up in Yorkshire and Birmingham. She studied music at Cambridge University and the School of Oriental and African Studies, and works as an ethnomusicologist at Trinity Laban Conservatoire of Music & Dance and as writer-in-residence with Aurora Orchestra. Her poetry has appeared in magazines and anthologies including *The Rialto, Magma, Oxford Poetry, The Best British Poetry 2014* (Salt) and *The Forward Book of Poetry 2016* (Faber & Faber).

The Rainbow Faults

KATE WAKELING

THE RIALTO

ACKNOWLEDGEMENTS

Some of these poems have been published in *Butcher's Dog, The Rialto, South Bank Poetry, Oxford Poetry, Magma, The Best British Poetry 2014* (Salt) and *The Forward Book of Poetry 2016* (Faber & Faber). 'Riddle' was highly commended in the 2015 Forward Prize and 'A Spoiling' and 'Hotel for Astronomers' were shortlisted for the 2014 Plough Prize.

BRIDGE PAMPHLETS

This is the tenth in a series of *The Rialto* pamphlets designed to cross the gap between magazine and book publication for new writers or, for established writers, that between collections. Previous pamphlets have been by Lorraine Mariner, Richard Lambert, Peter Sansom, Hannah Lowe, Jen Campbell, Janet Rogerson, Luke Samuel Yates, Laura Scott, Emily Wills and Richard Scott.

First published in 2016.

The Rialto PO Box 309 Aylsham Norwich
England NR11 6LN

© Kate Wakeling
The right of Kate Wakeling to be identified as the author of this work has been asserted by her in accordance with Section 77 of the Copyright Designs and Patents Act of 1988. All Rights Reserved.

ISBN 978-1-909632-03-5

The Publisher acknowledges financial assistance from Grants For Arts.

LOTTERY FUNDED

The Rialto is a Registered Charity No. 297553
Typeset in Berling 10 on 12.5pt
Design by Starfish, Norwich
Printed in England by Page Bros, Norwich, Norfolk
Cover illustration: Spaghetti Junction by Nick Stone

For T.M.B.

CONTENTS

Lore	12
Looking Glass	13
Moth	14
Lift	15
Snow Shirt	16
A Spoiling	17
Hotel for Astronomers	18
Watching One's Loved One Play the Piano/Scalp Scabs	19
Riddle	20
Apparition	21
White Story	22
Correctional	23
Trumpett CXXIII	24
Tarot	25
Tacit	26
He Isn't Johnny Cash	28
Gamelan Poem	29
In the Next Room	30
Pluck	31
Twelve-Tone Scale	32

LORE

Her stride says comet. Javelin-tongued,
she spits the locks off doors, skins lies,
furnishes dark shapes with a song.
When they tried to crown her,
she shot burning through the crowds.
Her gaze is thunder then a famine,
her voice a hundred golden coins.
Sometimes she erases a constellation,
pins the watchman to the ground
and drums up dawn with her fat clogs.
She sways to the cheers of long souls.
Her blood is a drawling highway.
She feasts on clay and thistles,
rides rivers, salts dreams,
mutters the rats to sleep.

LOOKING GLASS

Woman looks at mirror
Sees skeleton
Sees the beggared skull
Startles at her blank-boned future
Is dense with want for this scrubbed fossil self
Feels sticky breath of demon at her elbow

                              Skeleton looks out of mirror
                                         Watches woman
                                  Watches her glazed cheek
                     Wonders at the fallow of her peachiness
                     Is quick with fatigue at the slog of her pulse
                     Looses thrilled surrender across vacant ribs

MOTH
'And I.' (A Midsummer Night's Dream, Act III, Sc. 1)

Spirit of a common rate, I spent my fairy dues.
Squandered the lot on mortal grossness:
jewels, apricocks, toadstools, roses. Got lost
in cheap breezes, shot my pedigree
until, by some curt magic or other,
cat got part my tongue and the game
was up for a nigh-on silent sprite
with no place left to skim.

Now hireling of the bower, I am the rule of three
plus one, netted in this very long night
of domestic wizardry. I am that sullen
fungus who counts the syllables,
skulking in the others' ribbony wake,
serving up my quiet
while waiting for the act to lift, for day to break,
for the broom, the door, some unearned luck,
the chink, the wolf, the wasted brands' coy glow.
Out of this wood I do desire to go.

LIFT

At first we only thought it took its time,
an unhurried judder from floor to floor.
Yet on it slipped, on and down, until
someone hazarded an hour, a day, the week.

We practised the calendar, accrued bacterial patience,
our small ceremonies of panic giving way
to deep contemplation of the cardinal points.
We came to sing the increments, registering

the throb of the cable as our own exalted infantry.
When the year dropped, we cheered,
and as matters crawled from our hearts
so we bathed in sweet, dusty numbers.

SNOW SHIRT

Exhibit AOA 1842; Aleut, Alaska; Otter intestine, grass.

Cased beside a bearskin   and twin drums and other things

prized for holding their shape across   time   and water,

    this slips   the promise.

       Gut-heft is teased to   translucence,

shed skin turned out,   turned in,

an onion lens   for this widest glimpse of ice.

    It says:

be sparse.   Molecules   court us,

    do so little for us   in pleading   concentration.

      Do not understand the cold,

loose-leaf a way to   spring and forgetting.

       Empty   and go north.

A SPOILING

But you didn't see her, my sweet,
slaking her thirst on sailors' piss,
gutting fish with crumbling teeth
and supping deep on any hankering soul
she got her scale-spangled hands on.

You didn't watch her lug that crooked hip of hers
across the rocks to give each lunar tug the snip,
or hear her pike the wind
and bid it chime her ribs
to knell and knell the absent tide.

So when at last she dyed our day
in far-off greys, you only slept
your plumpest sleep
as I rose to meet that achey dawn,
slipping blankly through the open door.

HOTEL FOR ASTRONOMERS

The ESO hotel in the Atacama desert, Chile, is reserved only for the accommodation of commissioned astronomers.

We did our best to steal entry;
shouldering telescopes,
wearing faraway looks and starry belts
but the management turned us away, glassy-eyed.

Availing ourselves of a sun-fat afternoon for cover,
next we attempted the service entrance,
concealed behind a haulage of graph paper and lens polish
until the pale-faced man on reception pulled us up.

So we opted to gaze from afar,
tracking back into the sand to peer through tunneled glass
and view the astronomers' single-ringed squints,
the back of their ruined, white-struck necks,
the zigzag wonder of their dining room table plans
that shifted faultlessly as the skies.

By day, we weighed the shy laundering of their white coats,
tallied who was snoozing in translucent hammocks
or sifting the configuration of another's freckles.

The astronomers' acute interrogations of the time-space continuum
meant it was customary, we observed,
for quarrels to erupt over the hotel reservations procedure.

Sometimes, the low hum that rose from the plush arrowhead
of their single concentration
interfered with the television reception
and a lone astronomer with a hankering for Australian soaps
would ring the curiously soundless bell on the concierge's desk
asking for something to be done.

By night we caught the traces of their star-barks
and sized their comet-spying jigs,
buffered, as we lay in the saltgrass,
by the haphazard accord of hyperaridity
and the meticulous glint of land.

WATCHING ONE'S LOVED ONE PLAY THE PIANO/SCALP SCABS

Piano is your dear chink. Softest-centre,
it is where pleasure and piety kindle high findings,
a tidy, massive world that is all body/no body.
I am mostly not there when it happens.
Fellow percussionist, I blindly play the ruby
coalescence, thumb my rough drum's skin until
something *molto dolce* flows. I like the flush
that blooms during your brainwork.
I like your somnambulist page-turns
and that, when full throttle, you issue
a delicious forcefield which will not be breached.
I like too the meaty fidget that lurks always
in your fingers. We do not talk about mine
and their magnet work, the hot little nag
that is all attraction, pleading nail to skull
and skull to nail as it tracks its sickly axis.
Once, I knew my way around a keyboard.
Now, you know your way across my moon-head
and its *giocoso* sea of tranquility. These hands
have landed where they need to be.

RIDDLE

And how does it move?
Its fat, blind feet pound my hands.

What does it show you?
Murky gold; a rage; where the dust falls.

How does it conduct the light?
With shaggy beats of its careless head.

Where does it lay the curses?
In the thin waters; at the fireside; where the veins open.

What does it hold?
A casket of blue filament.

What does it wish for?
To heap its rough tongue across dainty machines.

How does its warmth persist?
Through the acute force of the hammer.

When does it march with a sombre tread?
When both the wells are empty.

Where does it sleep?
On my bed like a thief.

APPARITION

I'll be the ghost, I said,
I'll be the ghost,
and so I was
from that moment
only vapour,
taking the pale flight
from oar and gristle,
to admit an ivory culpability
and let my face peter out.

I thought it was bliss
to be the ghost,
going about my business
butchering the hymnal
with a tiny fork.

I found I was a fine translator,
as we ghosts so often are,
applying a glassy rigour
to impermanent tongues,
letting the fog run clear
to quench our punished thirsts.

But in the end I drifted
too long in the town square,
craving the mistress of the séance
in her fabled catchment,
she alone attuned to the rainbow faults.

I longed to craft an anthem in her name
and range across the greedy souls
to seize their tithe,
churn them mute.

But as I stayed,
so the hurly burly
stole into me as a cipher
and I sipped myself dry.

WHITE STORY

I am painting this bedroom.

I slather these walls compliant.

I am righteous to scold antique pinks,
to smack these princess tints with an assent of white.

I have come to know all my whites:
the coltish whites, flinching whites, demon whites.

I whiten this slab for our sweetmeats.

I streak the juice of our one white heart across these walls.

I scribe my deep white signs into these walls.

I find I have numberless white and noxious tongues:
I am a babel of whites.

I stipple casual futures into the pale, just as I fancy, and I watch them dry.

CORRECTIONAL

No flag: they keep a man on the roof
with a rattle in his throat. At his feet hang

the tile men, rain catching in their knuckles,
spilling down their backs and onto the yard

where a chosen two grip circlets of old net
and another gathers into a ball.

At night, the lucky half slumber on beds
of pale, assembled limbs while a man with

crooked elbows circles the time against a wall.
Each eats from another's clasped hands.

In the washroom, the mirror does his best.
Those here longest hook another to their heels

and gain a shadow.

TRUMPETT CXXXIII

Pegg my soul to thys.
Lett me committ meagre & fiery knowings.

I barrel through druds
as the druds they come
& my crux is that they liftt & weigh.

Decipher your own tricksy sond
& glugg the ear's every make.

Countt & cheer the gummy fungus
& all enemies of crustt.
Be an enemy of crustt.

Frolly with water & leafe
to sup each their bubbicles.
Be a silver fishe among every of the senses.

Flummox the panicky moth
to be heartened by the darke fix,
to be practised by the darke fix,
to be itched by the darke fix.

For time on time has seene me
& so, for time, see I thys.

Relatively little is known of the life of **Peter Chalf** (c. 1810 – 1879). Born in Truwerick, Cornwall to a family of blacksmiths, Chalf spent much of his adult life journeying on foot across Europe. Sometime in the late 1860s Chalf settled in the Norwegian fjord village of Knulvåg, where he lived as a recluse and began compiling his 7 volumes of 'Trumpetts' – short tracts on subjects ranging from arctic fishing to the nature of dreams. Chalf's writing is notable for its frequent use of neologism and its idiosyncratic spelling and syntax. This edition presents Chalf's text as found in his original manuscript (currently held in the Norsk Folkemuseum, Bygdøy).

TAROT

The man with the cards whittles doubt to art,
spits and trucks his way up the fat tor
of smalltime kismet, churning lost milk to tar
that is gold, as black is gold, as fortune is gold or tat
or question or answer or this sweet arcana trot
that hooks the Hanged Man and his Star to
a secret fold. The deck demands its agitator,
and the man with nimble lips builds that rot
because a life must sometimes beg to start, O
beg to end, O beg another to sculpt, to spill, to rat
on what will be will be, each creaking part to
tell or to be told, as chance is my spectator.

TACIT

Prospero: *No tongue! All eyes! Be silent.* [soft music]
(The Tempest, Act IV, Sc. I)

In the beginning came the hush:
nub of his rule, the anti-ruckus,
my quiet kept to forge his crown.
This was a daughter tutored mute,
speech no sooner to bloom than be swaddled.
He saw me stitch the peace deep into my cheeks,
gobble down the word
and keep my trap shut tight.

But sound was this one's ministry:
how he skulled and beggared,
how he wrought rule from stagnancy
to whip the heavens red.
To bid this child dumb was too brisk, too plain.
To grip his realm was to fix
and furnish a daughter with noise:
to make her sound.

And so, turning nine,
I woke to bells hooked from the hems,
bronze blinking at my ankles,
a daughter cast for the day as his chime.
The next morning brought looping strings
hooked across the arms, winds instructed
to duck through this, his prone little harp.
Before the third night sank
I caught his drift: speechless,
I was to take up the tune.

From here, I plucked gut strings,
puckered at trumpets,
trilled across flutes, pipes, keys.
Captive as an echo, I bred my faculties
as he sat deep in his chair
in blank pride, in his maestro's assurance
that he ruled and ruled and ruled.

And for a time I waited for an end,
for when he'd let the sounding stop
and bid me surface a thought.
Instead, I saw my skin begin to thicken,
drawing stiff across a ring of bones,
and I knew, in not so many beats,
I'd soon be just his drum.

HE ISN'T JOHNNY CASH

He's his own refrain,
walking the tightrope black
of the Northern Line
in his black coat.
He cuts up the carriage
with his honey croak,
with his magnet reek
of drink, snakes, loose change.
Dead ringer, music quits
his fingers like rust.
He's everything wrecked
upon everything wrecked;
use and danger
in neat, dirty echo.

GAMELAN POEM

Gamelan is thrust and tussle,
full-throttle hoot of smashed
tones. Gamelan is starburst
gumption. Gamelan is the
tinny thrill of reckless cheek.
It is soul music for chipped souls,
flinty song of the secretly unlocked.
Gamelan pushes its nose up beyond
deep motivation. Gamelan is sombre
thud of gong pursued by raging cloud
of bronze bees. Gamelan is the un-
shilly-shally, the hum and thwack,
the clobber and charge. Gamelan
is the zinger that bites twice, a naughty
tail on the make, of punch and wriggle
and sting and muscled zoom.

IN THE NEXT ROOM

you will casually sweat moss and sea salt. The trees' pumping hearts will soothe your shining troubles while, on the hour, pods of whales will drift overhead, casting their sincere shadows across your state of mind. You will find you have the bone structure for a French crop. Your dreams will be embroidered for you in silk minutes and when you wake, you will be encouraged to run that sculpted finger of yours along the threads and to marvel at the perceptive ochres, the hot, insolent purples. Cup a hand to an ear at any moment and you will hear your earthy, self-sufficient grandmother singing you a folk-song. The days will leak constantly into twilight and you will love that.

PLUCK

Tick-tock say so:
go or be goblined,
toe a bright step o'er trilling bricks.
Mind the gawpies, the slys,
mind that foul-lipped optic
in his crouch. Pad on
with teensy freight,
with pouch of uppity,
without peep,
trample it here, there.
Go quick
or be skimmed
or flicked.
Go quick
and be
bright
new
heap.

TWELVE-TONE SCALE

1. Jupiter's purr. Low creak of flourishing origin myths.

2. Gravity heard through an ear trumpet.

3. Rumble of large, unidentified footprints.

4. Thud of inglorious revelation.

5. Combined drone of all tuneless totems.

6. Murmur of healing wounds and old maps.

7. Anxious hum of arthritis in the family.

8. Yowl of shoplifting and widow's peaks.

9. White trill of unrequited love.

10. One-note song of grapefruit, awe and fanged monkeys.

11. Any kind of laser. The moment before falling of a ladder. Chlorophyll.

12.